Consultant Pierrick Picot
Managing Editor Belinda Hollyer
Editor Bridget Daly
Design Jane Robison
Sally Boothroyd
Picture Research Caroline Mitchell
Production Rosemary Bishop
Illustrations John Shackell
Tony Payne
Colin Rose
Janet Munch
Marilyn Day
Raymond Turvey
Maps Matthews & Taylor Associates
(pages 44–45)

Photographic Sources: Air France, BBC Hulton Picture Library, Camera Press, J. Allan Cash, Central Press, Martin Chillmaid, Citroen, Richard Clapp Photography, Club Mediterranee, Colorific, Contemporary Films, Colorsport, Commissariat-General, Anne Conway, Edimedia, European Parliament Information Office, European Space Agency, Mary Evans Picture Library, Explorer, French Government Tourist Office, Food from France, Giraudon, Robert Harding Picture Library, Hermes/Sally Stevens PR, Imperial War Museum, Keystone, Mansell Collection, Musee des Beaux Arts Lausanne, National Gallery, Popperfoto, Picturepoint, Presse Sports, Rex Features, Barrie Smith, SNCF, Uniphoto, Roger-Viollet, Frank Whitchurch, ZEFA

A MACDONALD BOOK

© Macdonald & Co (Publishers) Ltd 1973, 1986

First published in Great Britain in 1973 by Macdonald Educational Ltd

This revised edition published in 1986 by Macdonald & Co (Publishers) Ltd London & Sydney
A BPCC plc company

Printed and bound in Great Britain by Purnell & Sons (Book Production) Ltd

Macdonald & Co (Publishers) Ltd
Greater London House
Hampstead Road
London NW1 7QX

British Library Cataloguing in Publication Data
Tunnacliffe, Chantal
France.—(Countries)
1. France—History
I. Title   II. Series
944   DC38

ISBN 0-356-11512-7
ISBN 0-356-11513-5 Pbk

France

the land and its people

Chantal Tunnacliffe

Macdonald Educational

Contents

A land of many contrasts

A very spacious country

France is the largest country in Europe (549,000 km^2) and has a great variety of landscape. Mont Blanc, in the Alps, is the highest mountain in Europe (4,810m) while other parts like the marshy Camargue or the plain of Beauce are completely flat.

France's landscape can be divided into a series of 'threes'. It has three upland areas – the Armorica, the Massif Central and the Vosges; three mountain ranges – the Pyrenees, Jura and Alps and three lowland areas – the Paris Basin, the Aquitaine Basin and the Rhône-Saône corridor. It has some 3,000 km of coastline, bordering on three seas – the North Sea, Atlantic Ocean and the Mediterranean Sea. Much of this coast has fine sandy beaches. The longest river in France is the Loire (1009 km).

Contrasts in climate and vegetation

The climate in the north and in the Paris region can be very wet and cold (3°C in Paris in January – 15°C in July) but in the South (*Le Midi*) it is much warmer (7°C in Marseilles in January – 22°C in July). Because of the contrasts in temperature and relief, the vegetation is very varied too: apricots, almonds and peaches grow in the Rhône valley and mimosa and palm trees are common on the French Riviera and of course vineyards are found all over the south. About 26 per cent of France is covered in forest, especially in the Jura and the Vosges mountains where there are magnificent forests of fir trees. Near Bordeaux there is a large pine forest called Les Landes. The trees were planted just before the French Revolution to hold back the sands which were engulfing whole villages. In the Mediterranean south the land is covered by a low-growing evergreen scrub of pines, olives and aromatic shrubs which is known as the *maquis*. The high Alps and Pyrenees have large areas of mountain tundra.

Natural resources

Although there are many industries, especially in the north-east, the country is still the leading agricultural producer in Europe. It is self-sufficient in cereals, dairy

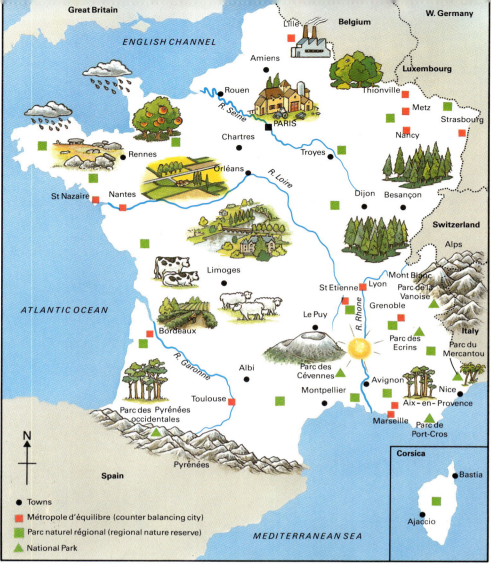

▲ France has the shape of an almost perfect hexagon and the French often refer to their country as *'l'Hexagone'*. With the exception of the north-east all the frontiers are clearly defined by mountain ranges or the sea and it is from the north-east that nearly all the invasions have come.

produce, meat, wine, fruit and vegetables. Market gardening flourishes in lowland areas and rice is grown in the Camargue.

Protecting the environment

Although France is a big country, the rapid growth of industry, the spread of motorways and much new housing is destroying a lot of unspoilt countryside. To preserve some of the best parts, National Parks have been created, for instance in the Alps, where eagles and mountain goats are found in great numbers and in the Pyrenees where you can sometimes see vultures and Europe's last wild bears.

▲ The marshland of the Poitiers area (*Marais Poitevin*) is also known as Green Venice (*la Venise verte*) for its many small rivers and canals which regularly overflow creating extensive marshlands.

▲ The Pyrenees are a high mountain range between France and Spain. The highest point is 3,400m. On the Atlantic side the Basque people live. They have distinctive red and green houses and often work as farmers and shepherds. On the Mediterranean side live the Catalans who, like the Basques, have their own language and customs.

► The Camargue is famous for its white horses, both wild and tame that roam over this flat marshland at the mouth of the river Rhône. The Camargue is noted for two other things: gracious pink flamingos and rice-growing. Unfortunately the flamingos damage the crop but rice is still important to the local economy.

► The Beauce Plain, south-west of Paris is a large region of flat land where the soil is very fertile. Wheat is grown on a large scale just as it is on the prairies of North America. The striking outline of Chartres Cathedral rises over the plain and can be seen for miles around.

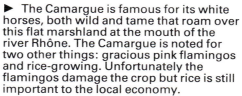

► France does not have much coal, oil or gas. This in part explains the French determination to build a large number of nuclear power stations. But natural energy from the tides can be made into electric power. The most successful example of harnessing the tides is the Rance power station in Brittany.

The French people

Paris and the provinces

The population of France is 55 million. About 70 per cent of the people live in the towns and Greater Paris alone contains about one-sixth of the entire population.

Before 1790 France was divided into 34 provinces. When Napoleon I came to power he split up the provinces into smaller areas called *départements* which were easier to control from the capital. Today there are 96 French *départements* and five overseas ones. France has always had a government that was centralized in Paris. This has meant that over the years people have flocked in to the capital to look for work or just to enjoy the 'bright lights' of a big city. Regions away from Paris were quite poor and isolated by the 1950s and something had to be done.

In 1955 the departments were grouped into 22 new administrative units called 'economic regions'. In 1966 eight towns were selected to become 'counter-balancing cities'. By giving these cities some administrative powers and also more industry and cultural facilities, more people are being attracted to the provinces.

The many faces of France

Although the old provinces of France now no longer have any real power, they are still important to the people who live in them because over the centuries they have developed their own customs, dialects, folklore, food and wine. Some even have their own separate languages, such as Breton in Brittany, Corsican in Corsica and Basque and Catalan on the borders with Spain.

There are not only French people living in France. In the 19th century, the country, like others in Europe, had many overseas colonies, particularly in Africa. In the 1950s many immigrant workers were brought in to help the expanding economy, mostly as skilled and unskilled workers in factories. They came from places such as West Africa, the Caribbean, Algeria, Tunisia and Morocco. Other immigrants also came from European countries such as Portugal, Spain and Italy and by 1972 there were over 3 million immigrants. The government restricted immigration in 1974.

▼ Pelota is a popular game in the Basque country on the border between France and Spain. It is played with a basket-like racket which is used to hit an extremely hard ball against a wall – somewhat similar to squash.

▲ The valley of the Rhône links two of the most important industrial centres of France: Lyons and Marseilles. It is here that a large number of immigrants have found work in such places as this nuclear power station.

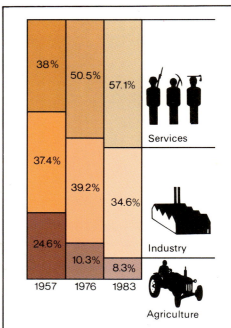

▲ In recent years the proportion of people working in agriculture has declined while industry and services have gained numbers.

▶ Martinique is a small tropical island in the Caribbean. It became French in 1635 and in 1946 was declared an overseas French *département*. The island is densely populated and a lot of people go to France to look for work.

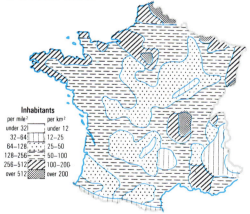

Inhabitants

per mile²	per km²
under 32	under 12
32–64	12–25
64–128	25–50
128–256	50–100
256–512	100–200
over 512	over 200

▲ There are on average 100 people per km² in France – one of the lowest population densities in Europe. But the map shows great contrasts between very heavily populated areas such as the Paris region, the North (near Belgium), the Marseilles region in the south and country districts or mountainous areas where there may be as few as 14 people per km².

▶ Near Quimper, in Brittany, you often see people in traditional Breton costume, like this woman. She is dressed in black velvet and satin with a tall, lace bonnet on her head. Brittany is well-known for seafood: oysters, mussels, crayfish and lobsters as well as a great variety of fish.

France, a cross-roads

An early melting-pot
The area which we now call France has been inhabited by human beings for about 35,000 years. The climate is good, the land fertile and it is a natural place for settlement.

The Celts from Central Europe had formed sizeable colonies in France by about 1000 BC. They were called 'Gauls' by the Romans who conquered them in 57–45 BC and this term is still used when we talk about the 'Gallic temperament' or 'Gallic humour'. The Romans stayed for 400 years. They left behind many buildings, roads and an idea of law and government which has been very influential throughout French history.

After the fall of the Roman Empire there were many invasions. Between AD 500 and 600 Celts from Britain, under attack from the Anglo-Saxons, set sail for what is now Brittany, where a language close to Welsh is still spoken. Norsemen from Scandinavia settled in the northern part (Normandy) in the 10th century and later, under William, they conquered England.

The most important of these invasions was that of the Germanic tribe, the Franks (from whom we get the name 'France'). Under their leader, Charlemagne, the Franks set up an enormous Empire (c. AD 800). At Charlemagne's death in 814, the Empire declined due to numerous invasions.

From about 1200, French kings, starting from a small area round Paris, gradually extended their kingdom. First Normandy was taken from the English king John. Then in the South they were soon in control of Provence, where a language close to Latin was spoken.

After that, France grew by taking over areas that had a very different language and culture: Brittany; part of the Basque country in the south-west; part of Catalonia, also in the south; Alsace where a dialect of German is spoken and part of Flanders in the north-east where the original language was Dutch.

By the 15th century France was almost the same country that we know today. Other peoples were to invade France, or use it as a place of refuge, but its basic character and boundaries were formed.

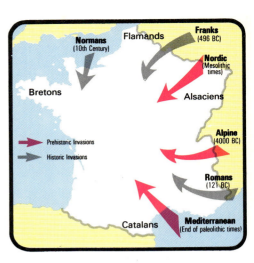

▼ Ruins of a Roman city in the south of France, at Vaison-La-Romaine. This part of France is rich in Roman remains such as amphitheatres, arenas and bridges.

▲ Prehistoric cave paintings at Lascaux in south-western France. These horses were painted in Late Palaeolithic times, about 20,000 years ago. The many caves found in this part of France have proved that France was one of the earliest human homes. The cave art found is said to be among the most beautiful ever discovered.

► Menhirs in Brittany. In the Breton language menhir means standing stone. They were probably erected in Neolithic times, about 4,000 BC. The stones stretch out in long lines and may have been the tombstones of important people.

▲ A piece of the famous Bayeux tapestry which tells the story of the Norman conquest of England by William the Conqueror. The Normans, Scandinavians in origin, invaded France in the 10th century.

► A statue of Charlemagne (742–814) who rose from being king of the Franks to become Emperor of most of Western Europe. At his death the Empire crumbled due to numerous invasions.

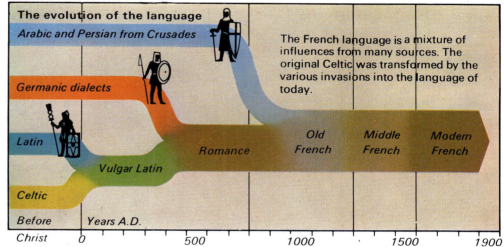

The evolution of the language

Arabic and Persian from Crusades

Germanic dialects

Latin

Vulgar Latin

Celtic

Before Christ

Years A.D.

Romance

Old French

Middle French

Modern French

The French language is a mixture of influences from many sources. The original Celtic was transformed by the various invasions into the language of today.

0   500   1000   1500   1900

▼ The medieval city of Carcassonne near the Pyrenees. The strong walls were needed to protect it from attacks by neighbouring lords.

▲ The French language is a mixture of influences from many sources. The original Celtic was changed by the many invaders into the language of today.

Louis XIV, the Sun King

▲ Louis XIV in magnificent ceremonial robes. His clothes were part of his status and brilliance.

King at 5 years

Louis became king when he was only five years old, in 1643, and reigned for 72 years – the longest reign in European history. At first his mother took his place in public while an extremely able minister, Mazarin (1602–1661), ran the country.

France's 'golden age'

In 1661 Mazarin died. Louis at the age of 23 decided that he was old enough to rule the country. At first he chose some very good ministers, especially Colbert (1619–1683). Louis had a few strong, simple ideas which helped him succeed for a long time. He knew that a king should look and behave like a king in order to impress his people. So he wore very expensive clothes, had hundreds of servants and entertained guests on a lavish scale. He encouraged artists, writers, painters, sculptors and architects. They produced work of such quality that his reign is still considered the greatest in French history.

Like most kings and rulers, Louis was afraid that someone, either in his own country or from abroad, would want to be king in his place and might even want to kill him. To stop his nobles becoming too powerful, he made them all leave their estates and come to live with him at Court. He couldn't fit them all in the Louvre Palace in Paris so he built an enormous palace outside Paris in a place called Versailles. He also involved France in expensive wars against neighbouring countries.

God's lieutenant on Earth

As he grew older, Louis began to think that he was God – 'The royal throne is not a human throne, it is God's throne'. But unlike God, Louis made mistakes. He could not tolerate any opposition. People had to do what he wanted and to believe what he wanted them to believe. He banned the French Protestants (called the Huguenots) and thousands of them were forced to flee to Britain, Ireland, Holland and Germany.

Louis' extravagance and his foreign wars finally ended by ruining the country and leaving its ordinary people in poverty. The seeds of the French Revolution were sown.

▼ The Palace of Versailles near Paris took 36,000 workmen and 50 years to build. But today you will find it empty. The contents were all sold during the Revolution. It took two years to sell everything.

▲ The King rewards his officers with the Order of St Louis. By giving these honours, he was trying to keep his nobles loyal.

► The siege of Valenciennes, 1677, one of the many wars entered into by Louis, which were ruinous to the French economy.

▼ On 24 August 1572 the French Protestant (Huguenot) leader, Coligny, was assassinated together with hundreds of other Huguenots. It became known as the Massacre of St Bartholomew's Day.

▲ The magnificent life of the King, the nobles and the churchmen was lived at the expense of the peasants. This cartoon drawn at the time of the 1789 revolution illustrates the crippling weight of taxation.

15

Napoleon, the little Corsican

The rise and rise of Napoleon
Napoleon Bonaparte was born in Corsica in 1769, the year after it became part of France. He was the second of a family of eight children. Like many Corsicans they were poor, but Napoleon won a scholarship to study at a military school in Paris. When the Revolution began in 1789, Napoleon was 20. He was at once sympathetic to the idea of the Revolution and was soon picked out as an outstanding military leader.

In 1794 revolutionary leader Robespierre was overthrown and guillotined. An uneasy democracy called the Directory was set up but a strong leader was needed to keep the country stable.

First in Italy in 1795–7, then in Egypt in 1798, Napoleon led his armies from success to success. Back in France he was greeted as a national hero and easily seized power in a coup d'etat on November 9 1799. He took the title of First Consul of the Republic but this didn't satisfy him for long and in 1804 he crowned himself Emperor.

Reforms at home
Napoleon is usually only thought of as a military warmonger, but he also tried to improve conditions at home by making plans to found the Bank of France, by regulating the collection of taxes by reforming the local government and legal systems and by improving secondary education.

The Napoleonic Empire
As a military leader, Napoleon's ambitions were boundless. Soon almost every country in Europe was under French domination. Solferino, Wagram, Iena and Austerlitz are now just names of bridges or metro stations in Paris, but they were the scenes of battles won by France that changed the face of Europe.

Soon, however, Europe began to unite against him. When he tried to invade Russia in 1812 he was defeated and exiled in 1814. He returned in 1815 to fight and lose his last great battle against the British and Prussians at Waterloo. After that Napoleon was sent into exile again, to the island of St Helena, where he died alone in 1821. France lost its Empire.

▲ It was not until 1840 that the body of the Emperor Napoleon I was brought home to France. The day of the funeral crowds of people watched a spectacular procession carrying the body of the Emperor to the Church of Les Invalides in Paris. There you can see the red porphyry tomb which encloses six coffins, one inside the other. The smallest one contains Napoleon's body.

◀ Napoleon at the Battle of Lodi in 1796. This battle in Italy, against the Austrians, and his whole Italian campaign were to reveal his military genius. The treaty which followed assured his fame as a conqueror and a peacemaker in the tradition of the Revolution.

▼ The Napoleonic Empire in 1810. At this time Napoleon was at the height of his power. In 1812 he set out to conquer Russia and his fortunes began to decline.

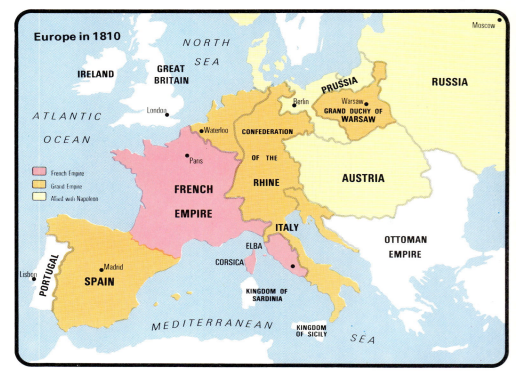

Europe in 1810

French Empire
Grand Empire
Allied with Napoleon

▼ The Battle of Aboukir in Egypt in 1798. Though Napoleon won the battle, his fleet was to be destroyed soon afterwards by Nelson at the Battle of the Nile.

▲ Napoleon in his coronation robes after crowning himself Emperor in Notre-Dame Cathedral in 1804. By doing so he revived memories of the Roman Empire.

▲ Napoleon and his wife, Josephine. They married in 1796, and were divorced in 1809, after a stormy but loving relationship. Napoleon later remarried.

▲ After his defeat at Waterloo in 1815, Napoleon was immediately exiled to the distant British island of St. Helena in the South Atlantic Ocean.

Revolution and change

A century of upheaval

After Louis XIV died, the power of the monarchy declined and France's economic crisis and poverty increased. Louis XV (1715–74) and Louis XVI (1774–93) tried to bring about reforms, but the cost of constant foreign wars made these measures ineffective.

In 1789 Louis XVI called a Parliament for the first time since 1614, hoping to raise more funds but the people (known as the Third Estate, the First and Second being the nobles and the Church) seized the opportunity to voice their discontent. This soon grew into open rebellion when the starving people of Paris stormed an old prison called the Bastille on July 14 1789. The French Revolution had begun.

The ideals of the Revolution were to establish a Republic giving 'freedom, equality and brotherhood' ('*liberté, égalité, fraternité*') to all the people. A National Assembly was set up and abolished the worst aspects of rule by the nobility and the Church. However, extreme factions took over and during a 'reign of terror' the royal family and hundreds of the aristocracy were guillotined.

The aims of the Revolution were not properly established for almost another hundred years, until 1871, when a stable government was set up under the Third Republic. From 1789–1871 France was rocked by a series of uprisings and rule of the country alternated between Republics and Monarchies.

Social changes

Due to the country's state of continual political and economic upheaval during the 18th and 19th centuries, the industrial revolution came late to France, not until the middle of the 1800s. After this time successive governments passed laws to protect the workers from being exploited, as up until this time working conditions had been terrible. Primary education was also made free of charge and compulsory for all children. The first socialist government in 1936 gave workers two weeks paid holiday a year and reduced the working week to 40 hours.

▲ The Bastille was built in the 14th century. It came to be used as a prison for important people. In 1789 the fortress was attacked, captured and destroyed by the Paris mob. All that remains today is a commemorative column in the Place de la Bastille.

◀ Jean-Jacques Rousseau (1712–1778) wrote a famous book: The Social Contract (*Le Contrat Social*), which argues against the idea that kings held a Divine right to rule. His ideas were important in both the American and French revolutions.

▲ This steel mill employed 10,000 workers in the middle of the nineteenth century. It was the time when railways were being built all over France and the steel works were kept busy producing metal tracks for the railways.

► King Louis XVI was beheaded in 1793. His death did not lead to the end of the Revolution: quite the contrary! A reign of terror began and hundreds of people were sent to the guillotine. The guillotine was a portable machine and it was carried round Paris like a gruesome travelling circus.

▼ During the Second Empire (1852–1870), Napoleon III's wife, Eugénie created a brilliant social life around her. Women wore sumptuous gowns and lavish jewellery. Their lifestyles were in stark contrast to the life and working conditions of the poor.

France in the twentieth century

Two World Wars

France's political history in the 20th century is dominated by its relations with Germany and by its attempts to hold on to its Empire in Africa and South-East Asia. At the end of World War I France had a few years of rapid economic growth but this came to an end suddenly following the Great Crash (the fall of the stock market) in the USA in 1929. The 1930s were difficult years. Germany under Hitler was again a threat to France and when war broke out in 1939 France was invaded and rapidly defeated. France was liberated in 1944 and the leader of the Free French Forces, General de Gaulle, became head of government (until 1946).

De Gaulle, a strong leader

After World War II one of the big problems facing France was the future of its colonies. The French lost the war in South-East Asia in 1954 and the same year found themselves fighting another one in Algeria. General de Gaulle was again called upon to deal with the situation and he became President of the Fifth Republic in 1958. Algeria was given independence in 1962 and France, which had been a founder member of the European Economic Community in 1957, soon became the fourth most important economic power in the world after the USA, Germany and Japan.

Towards Socialism

De Gaulle remained in power until 1969 and in the 1968 elections had an overwhelming victory in spite of the 'student revolution' of May that year. However he resigned the following April when he was defeated in a referendum on various reforms. Although Leftist political parties were gaining ground, the 'Right' remained in government for another 12 years until 1981 when the balance of power shifted to the Socialists under François Mitterrand.

A century of many changes

France's progress towards industrialization was a slower one than that of her European neighbours such as Germany and Britain. But she came out of the devastation of World War II with a new determination to modernize and economic growth and changes have been many and rapid. France is no longer a predominantly agricultural society. Some administrative power has been granted to the regions and industry, art and culture has spread to the provinces. One of the biggest changes is that women now account for about 40 per cent of the workforce and are being given equal opportunities in employment.

▲ June 1940. German troops march through the centre of Paris. The Germans occupied the North of France but left a puppet government in the south under Maréchal Pétain. General de Gaulle took refuge in London and organized resistance both inside and outside France. After the war was over, the Common Market was created chiefly with the idea of bringing France and Germany together so that they would never again go to war.

▼ President de Gaulle and Georges Pompidou when Prime Minister. Pompidou became President in 1969 and was considered by de Gaulle to be his heir.

▼ This cartoon of de Gaulle done in a street in Paris during the events of May 1968 uses a famous saying of his, "I understand you".

▼ François Mitterrand became president in 1981. He was the first socialist to win power in France for 23 years. His government nationalized the banks and major industries, imposed higher taxes on the wealthy and gave more money to help unemployment. They also began a process of decentralization, giving money and responsibility to local authorities.

▲ General de Gaulle was interested in making France strong in the world and rather neglected the need for reform and change inside France. At the same time he often seemed to treat the French as if they were children. Trouble began in May 1968 in the universities with student demonstrations and street riots in Paris spreading to large-scale strikes in industry.

▼ France was one of the original six members of the Common Market or European Community as it is now called. In 1973 Great Britain, Ireland and Denmark joined and in 1985 Spain and Portugal. Inset: the Chamber of the European Parliament.

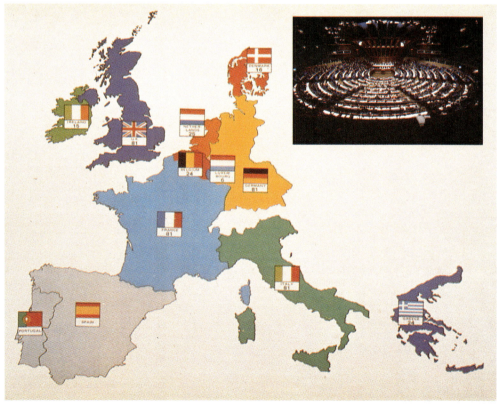

Culture and the arts

Royal patrons

The reign of François I (1515–47) saw a flowering of the arts in France. The king invited Italian architects, sculptors and artists like Leonardo da Vinci to France. They brought the latest fashions and ideas from Italy and deeply influenced French art. This period is now known as the Renaissance. Leonardo's most famous painting, the *Mona Lisa,* hangs in the Louvre Palace (now France's largest museum) in Paris.

After François I, the next king to have a great influence on artists was Louis XIV. During his reign, when nothing was too good or expensive, the arts developed remarkably: in music and ballet (Lully), in drama (Molière, Racine), in tapestry (the Gobelins Factory), in porcelain (Sèvres) and much more. Louis XIV's reign was an age of artistic magnificence.

The innovators

Another important period in French art came in the 19th century. Writers like Victor Hugo, who wrote among other works *The Hunchback of Notre Dame,* are read by all French school children. In music composers such as Bizet (*Carmen*), Berlioz (*La Symphonie Fantastique*) and Debussy (*La Mer*) are popular with music lovers everywhere.

The 19th and early 20th centuries saw the start of many new artistic movements in France which had a worldwide influence. In art there was Impressionism (Manet, Monet, Renoir), Fauvism (Matisse, Derain), Cubism (Braque, Picasso). In literature there was Existentialism (Sartre, Camus). In drama there was the Theatre of the Absurd (Ionesco, Beckett). In the cinema the brothers Auguste and Louis Lumière were the first people in the world to give a public film show, in 1895.

The arts today

All over France people are able to enjoy the arts. Since World War II, culture has spread out of Paris to the provinces. There are numerous festivals every year throughout the country: art, theatre, music, film and dance. Some like the Avignon Festival of the arts and the Cannes Film Festival have won international renown. New arts centres have been built in many towns throughout France and hundreds of small local 'community arts' events and groups have sprung up.

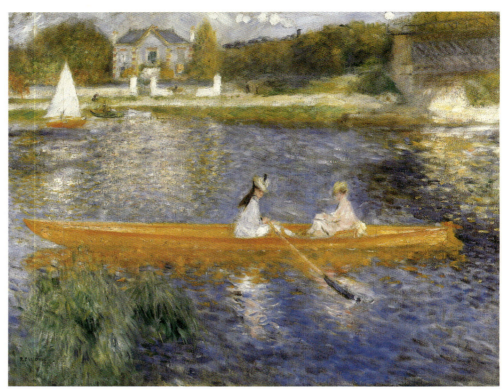

▲ Until about 100 years ago, most painters did their work in a studio, but Claude Monet and a group of friends (Renoir, Sisley, Pissarro) painted out of doors. They wanted to convey their feelings about nature. Water fascinated them most and this picture by Renoir is a beautiful example of Impressionism.

A scene from *Le Bourgeois Gentilhomme* by Molière (*left*) who is France's most famous dramatist. His work was subsidized by Louis XIV. His plays range from light-hearted farce to bitter criticisms of the society of the time. Besides writing plays he was also a leading actor. The French National Theatre, the Comédie Française is called Molière's theatre.

▲ The château of Chenonceaux is one of the many beautiful castles in the valley of the river Loire. It was built in the 16th century. Every night during the summer a spectacular 'sound and light' (*son et lumière*) show takes place. It tells the history of the château.

◄ In France comic strips are not just for children. Perhaps the most famous series of cartoon books, read by all ages, centres round the character of Asterix the Gaul, a brave little 50 BC warrior who refuses to surrender to the Roman invaders.

▼ During the Avignon Festival of the arts which takes place every year, the imposing, ruined, Pope's Palace is turned into a theatre. The massive vaulted arches of its courtyard make a spectacular backdrop for the plays and ballets that are put on there.

▲ The Pompidou Centre of the arts is several buildings in one: a library, a museum and an art gallery. People who don't like it call it the 'oil refinery', but its striking design makes it one of Paris's most popular attractions and it is now as much a part of Paris as the Eiffel Tower.

Invention, research and technology

Invention, discovery and research

What do air balloons, bicycles, pasteurised milk and the cinema have in common? They are all French inventions or discoveries and they are just a handful of the many remarkable scientific developments that have come from France. Every school boy and girl learns the name of Lavoisier (1743–94) who is the father of modern chemistry. He separated the main gases that make up the air and named the most vital one 'oxygen', but he wasn't given much thanks for his important discovery: when the Revolution came he had his head cut off! Pasteur was luckier than Lavoisier: following the great discoveries he made, the French government created a research institute (Institut Pasteur) with Pasteur as its head. Today this institute is a leading centre of French research in the fields of biochemistry and other biological sciences.

A national priority

Since 1981 research and development have been made a national priority. Certain areas have been singled out for special attention and effort in the hope that France will become a world leader in at least a few of them.

Biotechnology: this includes pharmaceuticals, agriculture and the new sciences related to genetic engineering.

Space research: in addition to the space rocket *Ariane* France is also developing satellites for telecommunications and other purposes.

Technological developments include:
Aviation: France's aircraft industry is very flourishing: airbuses, helicopters and military planes are exported all over the world.

Underwater exploration: there has for a long time been great interest in building bathyscaphes and other deep-water submersibles. One of these, a remote-controlled submersible called *Epaulard*, can reach 6,000 metres below sea-level. It is used in searching for oil-fields and mineral resources lying on the sea-bed.

▲ Marie Curie and her husband Pierre made scientific history in 1895 by extracting radium, which gives off radioactivity, from pitchblende. This startling discovery gained them the Nobel prize for physics in 1903.

▼ Louis Blériot (1872–1936) was the first man to fly long distances. On July 25, 1909, he crossed the English Channel from Calais to Dover in 1 hour 37 minutes. His plane, the Blériot XI, arrived safely except for losing a wheel on landing. He was already a famous figure before this flight, having invented a new type of light for the motor car. Several heavier-than-air monoplanes were designed by Blériot but all crashed. After his historic flight he continued building aircraft and lived to see the development of commercial passenger services.

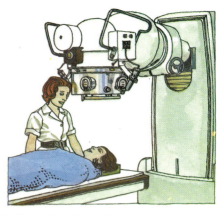

▲ Since the Curies' discoveries, radium has been used in numerous ways, especially in medicine. Here, for example, a radiographer examines a patient with a machine which makes use of radioactive waves, or X-rays.

▼ Two brothers, Joseph and Etienne Montgolfier were the first to construct a practical hot-air balloon. The first successful flight in 1782 took them 9.6 km.

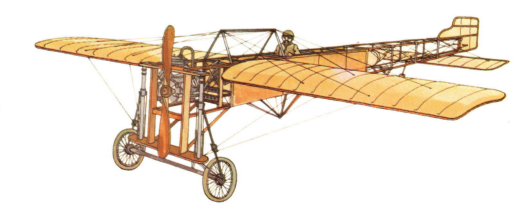

► Commander Jacques-Yves Cousteau is known world-wide for his exciting discoveries beneath the oceans. After graduating as an officer, he began a career in oceanographic research. He is the inventor of the aqualung, the diving saucer *Denise* (*right*) and an undersea laboratory. By making films and writing books on the exploration of the sea, he has done more than any man alive to popularize the subject.

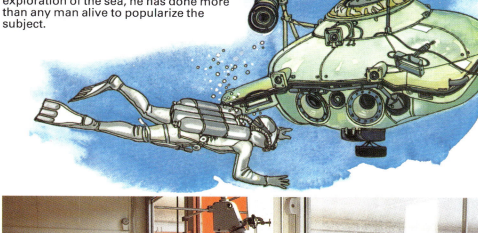

▲ Pasteur (1822–95) discovered tiny organisms or germs in milk, wine and beer which could carry disease. By heating these liquids rapidly to around 85°C the germs are killed without spoiling the taste. This process is called pasteurization. He also discovered an anti-rabies vaccine.

▼ When we think of space rockets and satellites most people only ever think of the Americans and the Russians but Europe too has its space programme. The *Ariane* space rocket is built in Toulouse but is launched in South America from the French colony of Guyana.

▲ Research laboratories today are full of highly expensive and sophisticated equipment which comes mainly from Germany, Japan and the USA. The French government is trying hard to stop France slipping further behind these three countries.

▼ Concorde, the world's first supersonic jet, was built jointly by the British and the French. Unfortunately it has never been allowed to fly over land at twice the speed of sound because of the noise it makes and so the plane has never really been a commercial success.

25

Paris, city of light

The heart of France

Paris is the capital of France and one of the best-loved cities in the world. 2,000 years ago it was a fishing village on an island in the Seine. It grew partly because it lies at the intersection of important trade routes and partly because an early king, Clovis, chose it as his capital in the 6th century.

Today the capital is the administrative head and political heart of France and the country's most important commercial and financial centre.

Conjuring up the past

A walk through Paris is a walk through France's history. The 600-year-old Notre Dame Cathedral, the Louvre Museum, the Place de la Concorde and many other places were the scenes of famous events; and all tell the history of the people and their times.

A city of contrasts

Paris can be all things to all people. There are the wide straight boulevards laid out by Baron Haussmann in the 19th century and the narrow twisted alleys of the medieval Marais; the fashionably expensive shops of the Faubourg St Honoré and the huge Flea Market at Clignancourt; the scurrying crowds in the metro and the casual walkers who saunter along the embankments; the rue Mouffetard with its noisy street traders and the Champs-Elysées where 'Important People' go to see and be seen.

The Seine, artery of Paris

Much of what is special about Paris centres on the river: the romantic quayside, the secondhand booksellers, the tramps who sleep under the arches, the glass-topped tourist boats (*bateaux-mouches*) cruising slowly along and the splendid buildings like the Louvre and Notre Dame floodlit at night.

► A map of Paris showing the principal buildings and tourist attractions as well as the various districts. Central Paris is divided by the River Seine into two distinct areas usually known as the Right (*Rive droite*) Bank and the Left (*Rive gauche*) Bank.

▲ Half-close your eyes and you could well imagine you were in New York. Steel and glass skyscrapers reflect each other and the passing clouds. Cars disappear into underground car parks or zoom along flyovers. This is La Défense, the biggest office quarter of Paris to which over 50,000 people commute to work every day. Virtually nobody lives there: after office hours it is like a ghost town. But the centre of Paris is only a few minutes ride away.

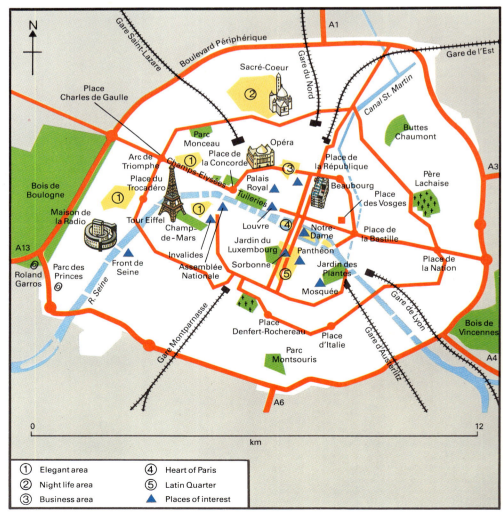

1. Elegant area
2. Night life area
3. Business area
4. Heart of Paris
5. Latin Quarter
▲ Places of interest

▲ Montmartre and the church of Sacré-Coeur. Until it attracted artists and poets, Montmartre was a peaceful village on the borders of Paris. Even today old windmills survive. It is now the centre of Parisian night life.

▼ A stone's throw from the fashionable and noisy cafés of St-Germain-des-Prés, you can find peace and quiet in a charming old square called the Place Furstenberg. The painter Eugène Delacroix (1798–1863) had his studio at no. 6.

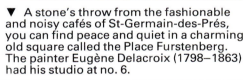

▲ The Eiffel Tower was built by Gustave Eiffel for the Great Exhibition of 1889. It is the tallest building in Paris (300m). Besides being a big tourist attraction, it is also a telecommunication centre.

Wine and cheese makers to the world

The most famous wine and cheese in the world

A bottle of really good French wine such as Château-Lafite may cost several hundred pounds/dollars and be sold at auctions like a painting! You can't imagine how anyone can actually *drink* wine that has cost so much.

If you want a good French wine you need to look out for the words *appellation contrôlée* on the label.

This means that the wine is from grapes grown within a specific area and may not be mixed with wine from other places. Good wine is often not only *appellation contrôlée* but bottled by the wine-grower on the estate. This is an extra guarantee of quality. Look for the words *mis en bouteille à la propriété* on the label and even stamped on the cork.

The two best wine-growing areas are Bordeaux for red wines, often called 'claret' in English, and for sweet white wines (Sauternes, Graves) and secondly, Burgundy which has wonderful red wines (for example Margaux, Beaune) and dry white

wines (Pouilly-Fuissé). And don't forget the wine that goes with every celebration all over the world – lovely, bubbly Champagne – the most French drink of them all!

General de Gaulle's proud boast was that France had 365 cheeses, one for each day of the year. Whether that is true or not, no French meal is complete without a selection of cheeses and a glass of red wine.

▼ Grapes have to be picked at exactly the right time. The wine made will be affected by the type of grape, the soil of the area, the weather and the skill of the grower. Even the best vineyards produce bad wine in some years.

▲ A wine château and its vineyard.

▲ The entire grape is used in the production of wine. Once its skin is broken, the yeast cells react with the sugar to make alcohol. Today most grape crushing is done by machines. The juice obtained is then pumped into vats and left to ferment.

▲ When fermentation is complete, the wine is put into bottles. Some wines such as Beaujolais can be drunk at once but others have to mature in the bottle for several years. Red wine contains about 10% alcohol and white about 11%.

The main wine and cheese products of France

Maroilles
Coulommiers
Livarot
Pont l'Evêque
Camembert
Brie
Champagne
Sylvaner
Munster
Muscadet
Chablis
Riesling
Sancerre
Vouvray
Port-Salut
Comté
Pouilly Fuissé
Goat Cheeses
Bleu de Bresse
Cognac
St. Nectaire
Cantal
St. Emilion
Emmental
Entre-Deux-Mers
Beaujolais
Médoc
Sauternes
Bleu d'Auvergne
Reblochon
Graves
Armagnac
Roquefort
Châteauneuf du Pape
Côtes de Provence
Jurançon
Roussillon & Corbières

▲ French cheeses are made in a vast number of ways which produce the variety which is without rival. They may be made from cow, ewe or goat milk. The most famous cheeses are matured over long periods, but some such as cream cheeses, can be eaten quickly. Mature cheeses can be divided into five types: soft-paste (eg Camembert), blue-veined (eg Roquefort), semi-hard (eg Cantal), hard (eg Emmental) and processed.

How Roquefort cheese is made

▲ Every region in France supports a large population of milk-giving animals which provide the raw material for cheese. Roquefort cheese is made from ewe's milk. This special type of blue-veined cheese can only be produced in the town of Roquefort in southern France. French law protects this right.

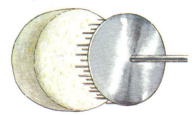

▲ The secret of Roquefort lies not in the actual making of the cheese but in the way it is matured. A powerful mould is injected into the cheese to produce the blue-veined character.

▲ Beneath the town are vast natural caves in which the air is cold and wet. The cheese is left here to mature slowly.

▲ The caves have the correct conditions to produce the cheese and nowhere else can these be exactly copied. Roquefort cheese is exported to all parts of the world.

The fashion magicians

The birth of haute couture

Paris is one of the great capitals of fashion but it was an Englishman from Lincolnshire, Charles-Frederick Worth (1825–95), who first had the idea of using real models to show the latest fashions. Worth became the dress maker to the Empress Eugénie, wife of Napoleon III and rich people flocked to buy his clothes. Fifty years later, a young Frenchman revolutionised fashion again. His name was Paul Poiret (1879–1944). He created modern fashion almost single handed. The styles and shapes he produced often seem modern today. But only a few people can afford individually made clothes made of the most expensive materials.

The perfume revolution

One of Poiret's brilliant ideas was to make perfume an essential part of high fashion. Since his time famous clothes designers have always had their own collections of perfumes: they are easier to sell than expensively designed clothes and they sell to many more people! There are new perfumes every year and another interesting change: as many are for men as for women! All with names like Dior, Lanvin, Chanel, Yves Saint-Laurent – each one of them a fashion house that has found perfume a real money-spinner.

Clothes for the masses

High fashion of *haute couture* has up until recently only been available to the very rich. But the fashion designers have realized that they can reach a much wider public by mass-producing their clothes. Ready-to-wear clothing (*prêt-à-porter*) has given everyone a chance to wear something with the name of a famous designer on it.

Paris, centre of luxury

Since the time of Louis XIV, Paris has been a centre of elegance. Some streets, like the Faubourg St Honoré, have dazzling shop windows filled with exquisite jewellery by Cartier, Boucheron or Chaumet, shops with fabulous crystal and silverware, names like Hermès (silk) and Vuitton (luggage), carry a French tradition of excellence around the world.

◀ Between 1910 and 1930 Raoul Dufy (1877–1953) produced thousands of designs for textiles. The silk manufacturers of Lyons made the material which was then turned into beautiful dresses and gowns by the fashion designers in Paris.

▼ *Hermès* is one of the most exclusive shops in the Faubourg St Honoré in Paris (equivalent to London's Bond Street or New York's Fifth Avenue). *Hermès* is famous for its silk scarves and leather.

◀ Women have always enjoyed wearing beautiful jewellery. At the beginning of this century, René Lalique (1860–1945) designed this delicate necklace. Later he turned to making marvellous glass objects and today his name is known for wonderful cut-glass and crystal.

▼ In spring and autumn, the great fashion houses put on a show of their designs or 'creations' for the next season. The designs are kept a close secret to prevent anyone stealing the ideas. Here, Yves St Laurent presents his new collection to rich customers and to the reporters of the fashion magazines.

Idées de Paris

DE EVOLUE, DES IDEES NOUVELLES NAISSENT, S'EPANOUISSENT... C'EST
NIE CREATEUR DE PARIS QUI CONTINUE. VOICI, JETEES SUR LE PAPIER,
QUES-UNES DE CES CREATIONS QUI INFLUENCERONT VOTRE SILHOUETTE.

1. — POUR LE THE. Tunique en
mousseline. Le devant est en-
tièrement travaillé de jours. —
Col, ceinture, jupe en satin. —
Mousseline: 3,90 m. en 96 cm.
Satin: 1,60 m. en 96 cm.
Patron Ringier en couleurs.
S i 3512. Taille 44.

2. — POUR DINER. Jupe en satin
(2,50 m. en 90 cm.). Blouse en
rubans de velours. (Métr. suiv.
largeur.) Pas de patron.

Although fashions have become
more casual recently, French
women still take a lot of trouble
to choose clothes and accessories
which mix and match perfectly.

From the 19th century to the
present day, French women
have been avid readers of
fashion magazines. Since
World War II there has been
an increase in the number of
fashion magazines such as
Elle and *Marie-Claire* which
have drummed ideas of
elegance into the minds of
ordinary French women,
enabling them to be as chic
as the women who can
afford to shop at the Haute
Couture houses.

The family at home

Strong traditions

Fewer people are getting married in France and people are having fewer children. This is true of most developed countries. Despite this, family ties in France remain stronger than in most English-speaking countries. French families get together not only for traditional family gatherings but also for holidays and other celebrations.

A home of their own

Traditionally the French live in flats in the centre of town or on country farms. However after World War II, many city dwellers moved out to the suburbs and now more than half the country's urban population live in new suburbs and housing estates.

Adjusting to suburban living has not been easy, as town planners in the 1950s and 60s had thrown up large soulless blocks of high-rise flats around cities with little or no social or leisure facilities. Planning is now better, with smaller, low-rise estates and nearby shops, schools, offices and sports and leisure complexes.

More and more, however, in the last few years, a house has come to be preferred above all else. This means moving further out to small towns or villages which have estates or *lotissements*, of trim houses with their own lawn and hedge and 'beware of the dog' (*chien méchant*) notice on the gate: the French see their homes as retreats from the world and tend to guard them like castles.

The further out of town people live, the longer it takes to commute in to work and this is changing French eating habits. Fast food shops are springing up in big cities because nowadays it is not so common for everyone to stop for a two hour lunch. But in the evening at around 8 o'clock, families with children get together for the traditional evening meal after the mother and father have returned home from work and the children have done one or two hours homework.

▶ Sometimes in the evenings the whole family gets together for a game of Scrabble. Scrabble is the most popular indoor game in France, followed by crossword puzzles, a card game called 'belote', chess and bridge.

▲ People in country areas watch much more television than people in the big cities. Young people mainly watch pop, folk or jazz concerts while their parents are more likely to watch the news, documentaries or cinema films.

▶ During term time there is not much time for leisure as every night there are at least two hours of homework to be done. Wednesday is a holiday but children have to go to school on Saturday mornings.

A growing affluence

The rapid rise in living standards in France since the war has meant that the working classes as well as the middle classes are now able to afford things like cars, TVs and holidays by the sea. Getting away for *le weekend* has become an institution for the middle class. The fashion for many city-dwellers is to buy an old run-down farmhouse or cottage in the country, and do it up. They will then cheerfully drive hundreds of miles each weekend just for two days away from the urban rat-race.

▼ French boys and girls are not always interested in sport though they do like very active holidays: skiing, swimming, sailing, windsurfing. Groups of young people often meet at each other's homes where they listen to music, read comics and talk.

▲ It is very unusual to find a house in Paris: nearly all buildings are split into flats. As a result there are very few gardens. Parks and open spaces are rare too but it is not difficult to get out of Paris and go to one of the nearby forests such as Fontainebleau or Rambouillet.

▲ These strange blocks of flats are in Créteil, just outside Paris. After the war the demand for houses was very urgent and the government had to build at great speed. Nowadays there are more detached houses being built than flats.

▲ You are just as likely to see a man as a woman doing the shopping in the open-air markets you find all over France. People go to the market for fruit and vegetables but also to buy delicious French cheeses, pâtés and a great variety of sausages.

▼ Another side of French home life: a farm in Normandy, one of the richest agricultural regions. Some villages, especially in poor and hilly regions, are very remote and do not even have the simplest modern conveniences.

▲ Bread shops are open every day from about seven a.m. including Sunday mornings! The French bread stick, called a *baguette* in French, is light and crisp but it does not keep. There are several other varieties of bread such as rye bread (*pain de seigle*) which goes beautifully with oysters, or wholemeal (*pain complet*). Despite having all this delicious bread, the French are eating less and less of it. In 1900 they ate over 500g a day and today only about 180g.

Eating the French way

Cooking, a national skill

In France, cooking is an art, a skill which is passed on from generation to generation. Food is one of the most popular topics of conversation, so much so that other people sometimes wonder whether the French eat in order to live or live in order to eat!

But eating habits are now changing. People eat far less nowadays than they did in the past. A main dish is now not always meat smothered in a rich sauce full of cream, butter or brandy. Even in restaurants simpler, healthier meals are served. The French have also become less snobbish about foreign cooking. The modern French hostess is nowadays just as likely to try out an amusing little Spanish paella or Greek moussaka she discovered while on holiday, at her dinner party, instead of a home-grown dish. But people will still drive long distances for the occasional gastronomic meal, and Sunday lunch is still, often, a large family affair.

The family meal

Although a young working couple without children will nowadays often just have a plate of pasta or pizza in front of the TV for supper, for families with children the evening meal is still the main meal of the day.

If there are guests, wines are carefully chosen to match the dishes being served. (When the family is alone, they drink the ordinary red wine.) The meal itself can be quite an event with four or five courses. On special occasions, or when there are guests, meals may last for several hours. Afterwards everyone relaxes with a cup of strong black coffee.

Christmas Eve and New Year's Eve are times when families get together. Both these celebrations are called *Le réveillon* and centre round a traditional meal, eaten late at night. It starts with oysters and is followed by smoked salmon, foie gras and turkey with chestnut stuffing. In case anyone is still hungry, the Christmas Eve *réveillon* ends with the delicious *bûche de Noël*, a rich chocolate cake (in the shape of a log, like a Swiss roll) which is decorated with little Christmas trees, Father Christmasses and snowmen.

▼ It would not be true to suggest that men do most of the cooking in France (yet!). But many men enjoy cooking and do it well. You would never say of a French man that he does not know how to boil an egg. After all, the great French chefs are nearly all men!

TYPICAL MEALS FOR A DAY

Breakfast:
7.30 a.m. (weekdays)
9.00 a.m. (Sundays)

Black or milky coffee or chocolate. Bread, butter and jam. Croissants on Sundays.

Lunch:
12.30 p.m. (weekdays)
1.30 p.m. (Sundays)

Artichokes vinaigrette, roast veal with cauliflower cheese. Crème caramel and fruit.

Tea:
4.00 p.m.

Bread and chocolate, or sometimes tea and cakes.

Dinner:
7.30 p.m. (weekdays)
8.00 p.m. (Sundays)

Onion soup, cold veal or quiche lorraine, salad, cheese and fruit.

MAKE YOURSELF A FRENCH MEAL

ONION SOUP GRATINÉE
(for 3–4 people)
2 tablespoons butter or oil
454g onions, thinly sliced
½ teaspoon salt
28g flour
850ml beef or chicken stock
6–8 slices of French bread
1 teaspoon olive oil
1 clove garlic
1 tablespoon grated cheese

QUICHE LORRAINE (for 4–5 people)
Pastry:
170g plain flour
pinch of salt
85g butter
28g lard
a little cold water to mix

Filling:
1 egg and 1 yolk
28g grated cheese
salt and pepper
70g milk
57g bacon, diced
1 small onion, thinly sliced
14g butter

VINAIGRETTE DRESSING
(for salads or cold vegetables)

2 tablespoons vinegar
5 tablespoons olive or nut oil
1 teaspoon French mustard
a pinch of salt and pepper

ONION SOUP GRATINÉE

Melt the butter or oil in a heavy saucepan and stir in the onions and salt. Cook on a low heat, stirring occasionally, until the onions are golden brown (about 20 mins.). Sprinkle the flour over the onions, stir and cook for 2–3 mins. Take off the heat and stir in the heated stock. Return the soup to the heat and partly cover with a lid. Simmer for 20–30 mins. Add salt and pepper.

While the soup is simmering, brush the bread slices with oil and bake, in a medium oven, until lightly browned (about 15 mins. on each side). Rub each slice with a cut clove of garlic.

Pour the soup into a tureen, put the bread slices on top and spread with grated cheese. Sprinkle with melted butter or oil and put under the grill until the cheese is melted.

QUICHE LORRAINE

Sift the flour into a bowl with the salt. Drop in the butter and lard and cut into small pieces with a knife. When they are well covered in flour, mix with your fingertips until the mixture looks like breadcrumbs. Make a well in the centre, add the water, and mix in with a knife. With your fingers, press the mixture into a firm dough, adding more water if necessary. Sprinkle some flour on a wooden board, and knead the dough until smooth. Put in the refrigerator for 30 minutes.

Beat the eggs in a basin, add the cheese, salt and pepper, and milk. Melt the butter in a small pan and cook the bacon and onions until just golden. Add to the egg mixture.

Butter a 7-inch flan ring or pie tin. Roll out the pastry and line the bottom and sides of the ring or tin. Fill the centre with the egg mixture. Bake in a fairly hot oven (Reg. 5, 190°C, 370°F) for about 30 minutes, or until firm and golden brown. This can be eaten hot or cold.

VINAIGRETTE DRESSING

Put the ingredients in a cup or small bottle and mix or shake well. Add to crisp, washed salad or cold cooked vegetables just before serving.

If you cannot get French mustard, English mustard can be used. You can add a pinch of sugar or fresh, chopped chives to this basic dressing. If you like, put a cut clove of garlic in the dressing, but remember to take it out to serve!

SOME FAMOUS REGIONAL DISHES

TRIPES A LA MODE DE CAEN
▲ This method of cooking tripe is the speciality of Normandy. It is a very old dish, said to have been eaten by William the Conqueror before he set out to defeat the English in 1066. The recipe includes Calvados, the fiery liqueur made from apples, and is traditionally served in this special dish.

HOMARD A L'ARMORICAINE
▲ The fishermen of Brittany are famous throughout the world for their catches of lobsters. This particular method of cooking lobster takes its name from the ancient name for Brittany, Armor. The sauce for this dish includes tomatoes, garlic, herbs, wine and brandy.

CASSOULET
▲ This is the great speciality of the people of Languedoc, in the south-west of France. It is a stew made from goose or duck, pork or lamb, sausage meat and white beans. The dish was originally introduced to the region by the Roman invaders, about 2,000 years ago.

BOUILLABAISSE
▲ The cooking along the south coast of France is very highly flavoured. This famous dish from the great port of Marseilles is no exception. It is a fish stew which can include as many as 20 different types of Mediterranean fish and shellfish, as well as tomatoes, garlic and onions.

Schools, tradition and reform

State controlled education

Although education was made compulsory a century ago, there are still in France a number of people who cannot read or write. Since 1959 school is compulsory between the ages of 6 and 16. All education is controlled by the state and most schools are free and non-religious. But there are many private schools run on a religious basis where fees are paid. A good education is considered important and French parents encourage their children to work hard. School hours are long and there is a lot of homework to do in the evenings. Although one mid-week day is free, Saturday morning is school time, so there is not much break for the weekend.

On the other hand the summer vacation (*les grandes vacances*) lasts for over two months and going back to school in September (*la rentrée*), is a very important event: children are bought new clothes, new satchels, and equipment for school and they meet their best friends again. Many children go home for lunch, but there are some pupils who have lunch at school and some who live in completely.

A changing system

It is not necessary to go to school until the age of 6, but most children go to play-group as early as 2 years old. This is a happy time, when children play games, paint, sing and make friends.

Primary school lasts for five years. Then children spend four years in a secondary school or college. Afterwards they either attend a normal school course at the *lycée* to prepare for the school-leaving exam called the *baccalauréat* or they follow a vocational training.

As long as you have passed the *baccalauréat* you can enter one of the 70 universities (13 in Paris). In 1983 there were 900,000 students in the French universities. But if you decide to study in one of the 300 *grandes écoles* you must first prepare then take a very hard exam before entering. When you have completed your studies in one of these high-powered colleges you can be assured of finding an extremely good job.

▲ A modern French school with pupils in the playground before the start of lessons. Many schools are however housed in very old buildings.

▲ A typical French classroom. By law, the number of children in any class must not exceed 35.

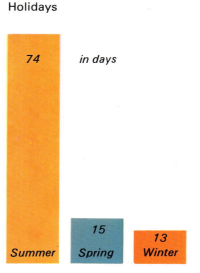

Holidays

in days

74 Summer

15 Spring

13 Winter

▲ The school year begins in mid-September after a very long summer vacation. As can be seen from the diagram other holidays are short compared with the one in summer. There are also brief breaks in the middle of each term.

The French school system

Universities and *grandes écoles*. Students have a choice between arts, law, economics, sciences, medicine or specialized studies.

Vocational training. A further one or two years can be spent in learning about a specialized profession which requires a detailed study.

Apprenticeship or on-the-job training. Skilled and non-skilled workers can undergo this training. Promotion comes with experience.

Lycée or grammar school. The brightest pupils will remain here until 18 and take a classical or a technical *Baccalauréat* examination.

Short technical school. Pupils may leave here at 16 or go on for a further year and obtain a diploma. They get general and vocational education.

Vocational school. All pupils in this school leave at age 16. They work for a certificate of aptitude in a certain skill or trade.

▲ France has a strictly controlled system of education. The chart gives a simplified summary of the present system. Though there are both private and state schools, the same subjects and courses are offered in both. After primary school pupils enter schools which suit their ability. Some will leave at the age of 16 while others will continue to 18. Some will go to university or take vocational training.

Primary school. This is compulsory from age 6 and pupils learn how to read, write and count. Here they will begin to be graded as regards ability.

Infant school. Though this early school is not compulsory more children are attending to learn basic skills like counting and reading.

How time is spent in school

	MONDAY	TUESDAY	WEDNESDAY	THURSDAY	FRIDAY	SATURDAY
8	French	Science	—	Maths	English	
9	Maths or French	Science	—	History or Geography	French	
10	English	German	—	Games	Civics	History or Geography
11	Maths	Gym	—	or Swimming		Art
12	L U N C H					
2	Gym	English	—	French	German	
3	History or Geography	French	—	German	French	
4			—	Maths		

▲ The timetable shows the weekly routine of a pupil in the 3rd grade (14 years old). One day each week is free – but the school week has six, not five, days.

▲ In the gymnasium. Sport is growing in importance in schools. Until recently, most schools have been poorly equipped with facilities for sport.

Sport and leisure time

Sport, a growing interest

Until recently the French were not a keen sporting nation. Today the situation is quite different. Amateur sport is very popular and French sportsmen are winning major competitions abroad. Many stadiums, swimming pools and other facilities have been built to encourage interest in sport.

Football is the most popular sport in France. It is played and watched by millions of people. The most famous teams are Paris Saint-Germain, Bordeaux, Nantes and Monaco. Recently the French national side has been successful, winning the European Championship in 1984.

The French enjoy cycling and you often see them at weekends training for races. But the biggest event of all is the Tour de France. Skiing has developed enormously since working people began to have five weeks holiday a year. The main ski slopes in the Alps and Pyrenees are easily reached by train and car. Other sports which have gained in popularity are sailing and windsurfing.

Not long ago only the rich could play tennis and you had to be a member of a tennis club, but today there are plenty of tennis courts and more and more young people play. They also watch the French championships at Roland-Garros in Paris.

Time off

Young people everywhere like to listen to rock music and the French are no exception. They dance a lot too and often go to parties called *boum* where they dance all night.

There has been a sudden interest in classical music, stimulated by an event which takes place on the first day of summer, called the Music Festival when people are allowed to sing or play an instrument wherever they like – even on the metro!

Café life is important in France, both for young and old. Cafés are a meeting place where people get together to eat, drink, talk, read, play cards or simply watch the world go by. Outside there may be a game of boules, played mostly by men.

The cinema is extremely popular and film actors and actresses such as Brigitte Bardot, Alain Delon, Catherine Deneuve and Gérard Depardieu have become as internationally famous as any Hollywood stars.

▲ Competitive skiing. Much encouragement and financial support is put into the training of competitive skiers. National and international competitions are very popular.

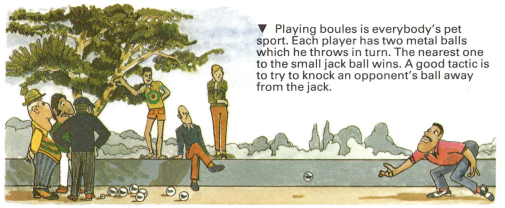

◄ Watching sport is the national pastime. In summer the stadiums attract millions of fans.

▼ Playing boules is everybody's pet sport. Each player has two metal balls which he throws in turn. The nearest one to the small jack ball wins. A good tactic is to try to knock an opponent's ball away from the jack.

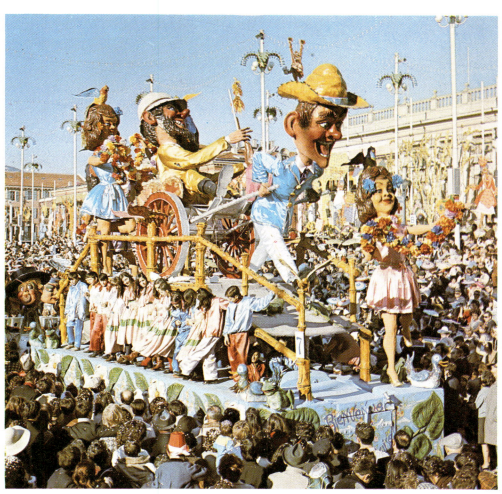

▲ Mardi Gras (Shrove Tuesday) carnival: in Nice flower-covered floats and giant figures process through the streets. In the evening, one of the giant figures is burnt on a huge bonfire. In most parts of France, on that day, children wear masks and fancy dress.

▲ The Le Mans 24 Hours race is one of the most famous car races in the world, a test of endurance both for driver and machine. It has taken place nearly every year in June since 1923 and every minute of it is reported on French radio.

▶ The horse races at Longchamp are an opportunity not only to try to back a winner but for elegant and fashionable people to see and be seen. The most important race of the season is called the *Prix de l'Arc de Triomphe* and it takes place each year in October.

Getting about and getting away

Transport

France's high-speed train, the TGV, is the fastest in the world, faster than the bullet train in Japan. The TGV goes from Paris to Lyons (400km) in 2 hours on a specially built track. A second line is being built from Paris to Bordeaux. The French railway system works extremely well and the intercity trains and the TGV are more like planes than trains with hostesses, air-conditioning and meals served at your seat. There are even special carriages with games for children.

It is said that the French are in love with their cars and they certainly use them a great deal. France has a good network of motorways but you need a deep pocket: they are all expensive toll roads.

The Paris metro is famous. Trains run very frequently. There are first and second class carriages and the trains make a little bleeping noise to warn passengers that the doors are about to shut. You can buy a single ticket but it is much better value to buy a book of ten tickets, a *carnet*. These are valid for both tube and bus. You can also buy a season ticket, *la carte orange*, so you need never queue!

The great exodus

For eleven months of the year, the French think about the twelfth month, when they will take their annual holidays.

Some people like skiing and go on holiday in the winter but most prefer the summer months. August is the big holiday time and many large companies close down for the whole month. In the big cities and especially in Paris, many theatres and shops close and the place is deserted except for tourists.

The great departure (*le grand départ*) and the great return (*le grand retour*) are like a national emergency. Millions of people leave by train, car or plane, all at the same time. This creates enormous traffic jams and congestion everywhere. Everybody races out of Paris and the big cities to the French Riviera or the Atlantic coast where they find more traffic jams and packed beaches. But as long as they eat well and get a good suntan, they return home pleased.

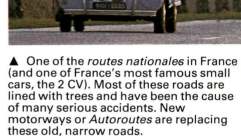

▲ One of the *routes nationales* in France (and one of France's most famous small cars, the 2 CV). Most of these roads are lined with trees and have been the cause of many serious accidents. New motorways or *Autoroutes* are replacing these old, narrow roads.

◄ London has its double decker buses but Paris has double decker trains! Every day 1,500,000 people travel into Paris by train to work. Comfortable modern trains run frequently and on time. This encourages people to use public transport and avoid the traffic jams.

▼ France has the most extensive railway network in Europe as well as the world's fastest trains, the TGVs. The French love their cars and the French Railways have to work hard to persuade people to leave their car at home and go by train.

▼ The small motor bicycle or *mobylette* is one of the most popular means of French transport. Young and old choose it for its convenience especially in heavy traffic and for its cheapness.

▲ When winter sports started to become really fashionable large new ski resorts were built in the Alps and in the Pyrenees. But some people don't want anything as energetic as skiing: they just want a nice suntan!

◄ About 300,000 French people go abroad every year with the Club Méditerranée. At these holiday clubs with a difference you can choose from nearly 100 idyllic locations all over the world. In some you stay in luxury hotels while in others your accommodation will be a Polynesian straw hut. All are famous for their sun, sea, sport and excellent food.

▼ French people take their annual summer holidays either on July 1 or August 1. Millions of people leave the large towns and rush by car and train to all parts of France. In August Paris is almost deserted except for tourists.

Gazetteer

Alps. 46 to 47 0N 6 to 10 0E. Principal mountains in Europe covering 130,000 sq. km. Drained by Rhône in France.

Alsace. 48 30N 7 30E. Region in the north-east between the Vosges and Rhine. For long part of Germany and again (with Lorraine) 1871–1919. Chief towns Strasbourg, Mulhouse.

Anjou. 47 20N 0 50W. Former province. Capital Angers. Anjou was under the English Crown in the 12th and 13th centuries.

Blanc, Mont. 45 52N 6 50E. Highest mountain (4,810 m) in Alps. Several sharp peaks *(aiguilles)*.

Bordeaux. 44 45N 0 38W. Prefecture of Gironde dept. on Garonne river. Chief port and commercial centre of south-west France. Wines famous. Pop. 640,012.

Brittany. 48 0N 2 10W. Caesar's Armorica. Former duchy and province. Settled by Celtic refugees from Britain in 5th century AD. Noted for seafaring, ancient monuments and folklore.

Burgundy. 47 0N 4 50E. Former province. Famous for wines. Settled in 5th century AD by Germanic Burgundii tribe.

Cannes. 43 35N 0 0E. Principal resort of Riviera, 25 km. south-west of Nice. Pop. 295,525.

Champagne. 49 0N 4 30E. District and former province. Famous wines are produced on slopes between Reims and Epernay.

Corsica. 42 0N 9 0E. Island north of Sardinia in Mediterranean. Area 8,681 sq. km. Pop. 240,178. Department of France though more akin to Italy. Napoleon born at Ajaccio.

Gascony. 43 40N 0 10E. Former province between Bay of Biscay and Pyrenees. Under English crown 1154–1453.

Grenoble. 45 12N 5 44E. Prefecture of Isère dept. and chief tourist centre of French Alps. Famous for kid-gloves; now also engineering and metallurgical industries. Ancient fortified city with cathedral (11th/13th centuries) and famous university (1339). Pop. 392,021.

Le Havre. 49 32N 0 5E. Important port at mouth of Seine on English Channel. Industries: oil-refining (pipeline to Paris), machinery, chemicals, flour-milling. Badly damaged in World War II. Pop. 254,595.

Jura. 46 40N 6 5E. Mountains along border with Switzerland. Highest point 1,723 m.

Languedoc. 43 50N 3 30E. Region and former province in south. Langue d'oc

is Provençal: oc='yes' in southern France.

Lille. 50 38N 3 0E. Prefecture of Nord dept. Great commercial and industrial centre. Fourth largest French city. Industries: textiles, chemicals, engineering, metallurgy, brewing. Flemish influence. Birthplace of de Gaulle. Pop. 936, 295.

Loire. 47 40N 2 30E. Longest (1009 km) river, flowing from Massif Central through Vichy, Orléans and Nantes to Bay of Biscay. With its tributaries, drains over fifth of France.

Lorraine. 48 58N 6 0E. Region and former province in east containing Meuse and Moselle valleys. Part of it, with Alsace, was incorporated into Germany 1871–1919.

Lyons. 45 47N 4 50E. Second largest city in France. Capital of Rhône dept. at confluence of Rhône and Saône rivers. Textile centre since 15th century, especially silks. Also financial centre. Founded by Romans 43 BC. Strong revolutionary tradition after 1793. Centre of resistance movement in World War II. Pop. 1,220,844.

Marseilles. 43 21N 5 22E. France's third city and principal port, on south coast 40 km east of Rhône delta. Originally founded c. 600 BC. Large trade with North Africa and Asia. Industries: ships, chemicals, soap, oil-refining. Pop. 1,110,511.

Massif Central. 44 50N 30E. Mountains dominating southern half of France. Highest points volcanic, eg. Mt. Dore (1,886 m) in Auvergne.

Médoc. 45 15N 1 0W. District in Gironde dept. in south-west. Occupies strip on left bank of Gironde estuary.

Nancy. 48 44N 6 10E. Prefecture of Meurthe-et-Moselle dept. and former capital of Lorraine. Iron and steel centre. Pop. 306,982.

Nantes. 47 17N 1 34W. Prefecture of Loire-Atlantique dept. on Loire estuary rivalling Rennes as chief town of Brittany. Important seaport with outport at St. Nazaire. Industries: ships, oil-refining, flour-milling. Edict of Nantes (1598) gave religious freedom to Huguenots. Pop. 464,857.

Nice. 43 45N 7 17E. Fashionable Riviera resort. Also textiles, paper, vegetable oil industries. Founded c. 3rd century BC. Birthplace of Garibaldi. Pop. 449,496.

Normandy. 49 0N 0 0. Region and former province in north-west. Norsemen founded duchy in 10th century. Battlefield in Second World War. Much dairy farming (eg Camembert cheese) and wheat. Capital Rouen. Ports: Le Havre, Cherbourg, Dieppe.

Paris. 48 52N 2 18E. Capital of France and dept. on rivers Seine and Marne. By far the largest city (8.7m.) with sixth of total population. Centre of

French communications and important European centre.

Picardy. 49 50N 3 0E. Region and former province in north Capital Amiens, centre of textile industry. Saw heavy fighting in First World War.

Provence. 43 55N 6 10E. Former province on Mediterranean coast. Home of Provençal language. Independent kingdom until 1486.

Pyrenees. 42 30N 1 0E. Mountain range separating France and Spain. French side noted for mountain torrents and spas and resorts.

Reims. 49 18N 40E. Centre of champagne industry in Marne dept. Magnificent 13th century cathedral (restored 1938). German surrender signed here May 1945. Pop. 199,388.

Rennes. 48 10N 1 41W. Cultural centre and former capital of Britanny. Badly damaged in great fire 1720 and World War II. Pop. 234,418.

Rhône. 45 58N 4 35E. One of chief European rivers. Rises in Switzerland, flowing west to Lyons, then south to Mediterranean. With its most important tributary, the Saône, it has been the major line of communication between the north and south of France for centuries.

Rouen. 49 28N 1 7E. Former capital of Normandy. Old quarter of 'the Gothic city' largely destroyed in 2nd World War. William the Conqueror died and Joan of Arc burned here. Pop. 379,879.

St. Étienne. 43 12N 1 30W. On second largest coalfield in France. Iron, steel and silk produced. Pop. 317,228.

Seine. 48 57N 2 25E. Third longest river but first in economic importance. Rises 28 km. north-west of Dijon; meanders through Paris and on to English Channel. Canals link it to the Meuse, Rhône, Loire, Rhine and Scheldt. 775 km. long.

Strasbourg. 48 35N 7 46E. Principal inland port on Rhine and Ill rivers. Business and cultural centre of Alsace. Notable cathedral. Headquarters of the Council of Europe. Pop. 373,470.

Toulouse. 43 37N 1 18E. Former capital of Languedoc between Pyrenees and Massif Central. 2nd oldest university (1230). Pop. 541,271.

Tours. 47 24N 0 41E. Prefecture of Indre-et-Loire dept. and manufacturing and tourist centre. Near here Charles Martel won historic victory over Moors in 732. Pop. 262,786.

Valenciennes. 50 20N 3 32E. Coal-mining and industrial town in Nord dept. near Lille on river Escaut (Scheldt). Pop. 349,505.

Vosges. 48 20N 7 0E. Mountains near Franco-German border resembling Black Forest on opposite (German) side of Rhine. Highest point 1,421 m.

Index

FRANCE · Political

Cities and Towns

International Boundaries	Département Boundaries	
Railways	Airports	⊛
Motorways	Canals	

Départements in the Paris region

1 YVELINES	4 HAUTS-DE-SEINE
2 VAL d'OISE	5 SEINE-ST. DENIS
3 ESSONNE	6 VILLE DE PARIS
	7 VAL-DE-MARNE

1 : 5 000 000

0 20 40 60 80 miles
0 40 80 120 kilometres

Projection: Conical with 2 standard parallels

North Sea

WALES
ENGLAND
St. George's Channel
Bristol Channel
English Channel
Channel Is.
Straits of Dover

NETHERLANDS
BELGIUM
WEST GERMANY
LUXEMBOURG
SWITZERLAND
ITALY
SPAIN
ANDORRA

MEDITERRANEAN SEA
Gulf of Lions

Départements

PAS DE CALAIS
NORD
SOMME
AISNE
ARDENNES
MEURTHE ET MOSELLE
MOSELLE
MEUSE
BAS RHIN
SEINE MARITIME
OISE
MARNE
VOSGES
HAUTE MARNE
HAUTE RHIN
MANCHE
CALVADOS
EURE
PARIS
SEINE ET MARNE
AUBE
HAUTE SAÔNE
BELFORT
ORNE
EURE ET LOIR
YONNE
CÔTE D'OR
DOUBS
CÔTES DU NORD
FINISTÈRE
ILLE ET VILAINE
MAYENNE
SARTHE
LOIRET
NIÈVRE
SAÔNE ET LOIRE
JURA
MORBIHAN
LOIRE ATLANTIQUE
MAINE ET LOIRE
INDRE ET LOIRE
ET CHER
CHER
ALLIER
RHÔNE
AIN
HAUTE SAVOIE
VENDÉE
DEUX-SÈVRES
VIENNE
INDRE
CREUSE
PUY DE DOME
LOIRE
ISÈRE
SAVOIE
CHARENTE MARITIME
CHARENTE
HAUTE VIENNE
CORRÈZE
HAUTE LOIRE
ARDÈCHE
DRÔME
HAUTES-ALPES
GIRONDE
DORDOGNE
LOT
CANTAL
LOZÈRE
GARD
VAUCLUSE
ALPES DE HAUTE PROVENCE
ALPES MARITIMES
LOT ET GARONNE
AVEYRON
BOUCHES DU RHÔNE
VAR
LANDES
TARN ET GARONNE
TARN
HÉRAULT
MONACO
GERS
HAUTE GARONNE
AUDE
PYRÉNÉES ATLANTIQUES
HAUTE PYRÉNÉES
ARIÈGE
PYRÉNÉES ORIENTALES
Canal du Midi

Cities

Stoke-on-Trent, Nottingham, BIRMINGHAM, Coventry, Northampton, Peterborough, Norwich, Great Yarmouth, Worcester, Cambridge, Ipswich, Gloucester, Oxford, Luton, LONDON, Swansea, Cardiff, Bristol, Reading, Maidstone, Exeter, Southampton, Bournemouth, Portsmouth, Plymouth

Alkmaar, Haarlem, Amsterdam, Zwolle, Enschede, Osnabrück, Herford, The Hague, Rotterdam, Apeldoorn, Arnhem, Münster, Bielefe, Schiedam, Dordrecht, Nijmegen, Oberhausen, Gelsenkirchen, Dortmund, Breda, Tilburg, Duisberg, Essen, Wuppertal, Eindhoven, Krefeld, M. Gladbach, Düsseldorf, Remscheid, Ostend, Bruges, Antwerp, Mechelen, Maastricht, Aachen, Cologne, Ghent, BRUSSELS, Leuven, Liège, Bonn, Koblenz, Giess, Calais, Tourcoing, Lille, Roubaix, Namur, Charleroi, Wiesbaden, Mainz, Darm, Man, Boulogne, Lens, Mons, Luxemburg, Kaiserslautern, Saarbrücken, Heid, Montreuil, Valenciennes, Karl., Stut, Dieppe, Abbeville, Arras, Reims, Verdun, Metz, Nancy, Strasbourg, Fran, Offe, Amiens, Châlons, Cherbourg, Le Havre, Rouen, Epinal, Mulhouse, Freiburg, Caen, Versailles, Troyes, Belfort, Basle, Zü, Brest, Rennes, Chartres, Orléans, Dijon, Besançon, Chaux de Fonds, Bern, Luzern, Le Mans, Bourges, Nevers, Le Creusot, Châlon, Lausanne, St. Nazaire, Nantes, Angers, Tours, Geneva, St. Quentin, La Rochelle, Rochefort, Limoges, Vichy, Clermont Ferrand, Lyons, St. Étienne, Grenoble, TURIN, Allessar, Poitiers, Angoulême, Périgueux, Bordeaux, Avignon, Nîmes, Montpellier, Béziers, Sète, Narbonne, Marseilles, Toulon, Cannes, Nice, Monte Car, Santander, San Sebastian, Biarritz, Bilbao, Bayonne, Pau, Toulouse, Vitoria, Pamplona, Perpignan, Burgos, Logroño, Huesca, Gerona, Palencia, Soria, Zaragoza, Lérida, Valladolid, Tarragona, Segovia, Sabadell, Badalona, Hospitalet, BARCELONA, Guadalajara, Tortosa, MADRID

West from Greenwich 0 East from Greenwich

On same scale as main map

CORSICA
Bastia
Ajaccio
Bonifacio